BENEATH THE BANYAN TREE

Mannika Solanki

BlueRose Publishers

First Published in March 2021

ISBN: 978-93-5427-441-1

BLUEROSE PUBLISHERS

www.bluerosepublishers.com

info@bluerosepublishers.com

+91 8882 898 898

Cover Design:

Disha Bothra

Typographic Design:

Tanya Raj Upadhyay

Distributed by: BlueRose, Amazon, Flipkart, Shopclues

CONTENTS

UNDEFINED 1
A NIGHT OF ILLUSIONS 2
DREAM IN SLOW MOTION 4
AN UNBREAKABLE HEART 5
OH WONDER 7
HE SMILES FOR ME 8
MY GALAXY 9
ONCE UPON A BOY 10
DWELL NOT ON LOVE 11
THE SOUND OF HEARTBREAK 13
THEM 15
UNAVAILABLE 17
WHEN 19
THE NIGHT YOU BROKE MY HEART 21
PAPER-CUT 23
SEPARATION 24
TEARY EYED 25
THE FIRST AND THE LAST 26
COME BACK 27
ETERNAL 28
FALLING 29
NEVER 30
OBLIGATIONS 31

SHADOW....32
NAKED....33
UNHEARD....35
TORRENTIAL TORMENT....36
HEART OF SHAME....37
IF....38
TASTED RED....40
SHE....42
STEPS – A RHYME....43
WHISPERS....44
VIRGIN....45
LOVE AGAIN....46
SONGBIRD....47
SEASONS' MEETINGS....48
ORIENTAL BLOOM....50
BENEATH THE BANYAN TREE....51
HEAVEN....53
LOVERS' STORY....54

UNDEFINED

It was neither day nor night
Neither light nor dark,

It was neither winter nor summer
Neither cold nor hot,

It was neither autumn nor deluge
No leaf nor rain did fall,

It was neither then nor now
Time had simply stopped,

It was neither fast nor slow
I could just not feel my heart,

I was neither happy nor sad
What I felt I could not tell,

It was all undefined
When you kissed me the first time.

A NIGHT OF ILLUSIONS

I went to bed at nine last night,
Woke up in a pitch-black room,
Seated on a red sofa-chair next to you.

I opened my eyes slowly,
Let the vastness of the dark seep in,
Looked to the right;
Saw a dazzling shimmer,
The shimmer was your eyes.

In the distance I looked again,
Felt a deep, seeping pain,
I thought I lost you;
Then shone a bright white light,
The bright light was your smile.

Looked, now, up ahead,
At the empty space so wide,
I picked up my hand to touch it,
You held my hand tight;
Reassured, you were by my side.

Grey smoke filled my lungs,
I could not feel my heart,
Or you by my side;
You'd left in a haze,
Taken my heart away.

It was a night of illusions,
An illusion of love,
Of you by my side;
Of those shimmering eyes,
That big bright smile.

It was a night of illusions,
Of finding forever,
Of losing my heart,
Keeping in its place
Yours instead.

It was a night of illusions,
What woke me up from it
Was your heartbeat next to mine.

DREAM IN SLOW MOTION

It was a dream in slow motion,
Haphazard memories moving slowly,
Through my veins, to my head.

In slow motion, it came to my eyes hence,
Then slowly moved to my lips,
That, even in my sleep, gave out a sigh.

Just before I could reach out to hold it,
Not slowly this time, it slipped,
As I sat up, awake, with open eyes.

AN UNBREAKABLE HEART

Three layers or more, of rock-solid ice
That is what I wrapped my heart with
This formula, I thought, was full-proof.

Patience, a lot of it, warmth and love
He melted it slowly, layer after layer
This formula, he knew, was full-proof

The shivers I felt, with every warm touch
The shivers I felt, with every melting layer
That formula was full-proof, I thought

The shivers he felt, from my icy heart
The shivers he felt, with every melting layer
The formula was full-proof, he knew

The ice melted one day, by his warmth
He touched my now exposed heart
My formula failed, it wasn't full-proof

My heart radiated a new glow,
A warmth I had not known before
My formula had failed, but it felt good

He took my heart and kept it in his
To hold and protect this fragile thing
No formula for this but one, said he

A layer of my heart over yours,
To break yours, break mine first,
Love, the only formula that is full-proof.

OH WONDER

Wonder it was how you loved me;
When I did not seem worthy,
Wonder it was how you stayed;
When all else frayed.

Wonder it was that you saw me;
For who I could be,
When all everyone else saw;
Was only who I had been.

Wonder it was indeed;
That you held me,
When I had wanted you;
To want to let go.

Wonder it was that you loved me;
When I could not love myself,
Wonder it was that I loved you;
That then I loved myself too.

HE SMILES FOR ME

He sits alone in the garden,
Thinking to himself;
When the leaves would shed,
Give the branches some relief.

It seems it has been long,
That someone did appreciate him;
He's a lonely boy,
In love, now, he doesn't believe.

Life's given him his share of thorns,
You can see the scars on his punctured skin;
People say he's a bitter lad,
But, he smiles for me.

MY GALAXY

You are the planet that I live on;
The air that I breathe,

You are the star that I
See before I close my eyes;
The sun that I see when
I open them in the morning,

You are the moon
That comes in my dream;
The black hole
I wish to drown in,

You are not just my star, my super-guy;
You are my galaxy!

ONCE UPON A BOY

A boy I liked once,
With stars in his eyes,
The sun in his smile.

He lived like there's no tomorrow,
Singing and dancing with him,
You'd forget all your sorrow.

A boy I liked once,
With a strut in his gait,
Hair so shiny and straight.

He made you feel wonderful,
A great company to be with,
With him you'd feel all calm and cool.

A boy I liked once,
Got super-good grades.
Of all the people I worked with,
He was my favourite.

I liked him once,
He once liked me too.
But time ran out on us,
Too fast and too soon.

DWELL NOT ON LOVE

Dwell not on the feeling of love,
Let it come and go, as it does;
When it's there, you'll see spring in winter,
When it's gone, winter will prick like a
splinter.

Dwell not on the longing for love,
Let it come and go, as it does;
When in your heart, you will feel strong,
When in your mind, you will feel worn.

Dwell not on the object of your love,
Let him come and go, as he does;
When in his arms, you will feel meek,
When away from him, you will feel weak.

Dwell not on the sorrow of love,
Let it come and go, as it does;
When in you, it will make you sombre,
When it leaves, it'll leave you humbler.

Dwell not on the joy of love,
Let it come and go, as it does;
When it fills you, rejoice and share,
When it leaves you, still don't despair.

Dwell not on the tidings of love,
Let it come and go, as it does;
For love can neither be created nor destroyed,
It's a feeling that travels between your heart & mine.

THE SOUND OF HEARTBREAK

What is the sound of a heartbreak like?

It is heard in the single long sigh
when you look at the erstwhile
object of your affection.

It is heard under the breath
of that single smile you forge,
when asked if you ever loved someone.

It is heard in that lonely sniff,
when no-one comes to wipe off
the tears that that one person gave.

It is heard in the silence of
those heavy eyes, that dare not see
anyone now in a similar way.

It is heard in the bland kisses
exchanged with strangers, never
having courage again to fall in love.

It is heard in the painful plea
of a new lover, why is it that you
can't love them the same way?

It is heard in the sobs of another
broken heart, the one you broke;
because yours wasn't ready for it yet.

THEM

His dark brown eyes,
Her deep light ones.

His strong sweet lips,
Her soft full ones.

His big thick nose,
Her small fragile one.

His hands, strong, big,
Her hands, strong, thin.

His neck, the Adam's Apple,
Her neck, the show of the mole.

His eyebrows, thick, in a line,
Her eyebrows, thick and fine.

His lashes, never noticed,
Hers, couldn't stop playing with.

His short hair, ran through my fingers,
Her long locks, I couldn't stop looking at.

His face, and how it filled my hands,
Her face, so small, the grip was perfect.

His chest, with the hint of hair,
Her beautiful bare breasts.

His wide, strong shoulders,
Hers soft, dependable.

His protective embrace,
Her comforting cuddle.

His smile said it all,
Her smile left it all unsaid.

UNAVAILABLE

I told my friend I met someone,
he asked me if it was dark;
If there was music, dancing;
perhaps alcohol involved?

I told him yes, I guess
the situation tricked me into it,
He asked me to meet in
broad daylight; I complied.

I met her on a bright sunny day;
my feelings for her remained the same.

I asked my friend, "what now?"
He suggested I meet her once again,
at night, without alcohol.

I met her in the moonlight;
the night was dark and still,
She smiled & waved,
and from a distance,
I could hear a violin.

I asked my friend, "dude, what next?"
He said, "meet her in
the inconvenient Mumbai rains."

I met her on a busy road,
covered in muddy puddles,
It was evening or noon,
who could tell;
it was the gloomiest of weathers.

She looked disturbed,
perhaps it worked;
I would now know something
about her that'd help me get over.

She complained about the weather,
the muddy Mumbai puddles,
I could see the anger building up.

But, sigh, the anger also, to me,
looked freakishly adorable.
I complained to my friend
that nothing seemed to work,

Exhausted he asked,
"why don't you two just date?"
To which I replied,
"because she's committed
and completely unavailable."

WHEN

When I would look at you,
look at me and smile,
My heart would skip a beat,
perhaps even stop a while;
Am glad we don't look at
each other like that anymore,
I couldn't afford to feel
so helpless as I felt before.

When you would look into
my eyes and not say a word,
A current would run through my spine
and get me all charged up;
I can't now, gather the courage
to look into those eyes of yours,
How depleting it was, each time
to look and be provoked.

When you would sit next to me
and take my hand in yours,
Time seemed stopped, even as
the sun made way for the stars;
I keep my hands close now, and
keep moving ahead with pride,
How far behind I was left,
sitting hand-in-hand by your side.

When you would lie beside me
and breathe deeply in your sleep,
A sigh would escape my mouth,
I'd hold my breath to hear you breathe;
Am glad I sleep alone tonight,
and so I sleep just fine,
How exhausting it was to watch
you sleep, and instead lose mine.

When we kissed, we kissed
each-other repeatedly,
My heart, each time, would sink,
filled up to the brink;
I'd have kissed you still, but am glad
you never again kissed me back,
For how petrifying it was to hear my
heart beat so, as if having a heart-attack.

THE NIGHT YOU BROKE MY HEART

I was lonely when you approached me,
Unsure when you walked me to the rooftop.

I was weak when you took my hand in yours,
Trembled as you pressed it against your heart.

I was lost when you looked into my eyes,
Smitten by your bright, beautiful smile.

I was looking as the sun kissed your skin,
Wishing that it had instead been me.

I was hoping it was my sweetest dream,
When you leaned in and kissed my cheek.

I was praying the day would never end,
As the Sun began retiring to its den.

I looked at the stars then looked at you,
You were the prettiest thing I knew.

I sat there for hours only with you,
As we talked, the time just flew.

I leaned to kiss your enticing lips,
To my surprise you did not resist.

I was in love, now I was sure,
You said it was friendship, nothing more.

PAPER-CUT

You were a book I started to read,
You let yourself open-up to me.

As I turned and explored each chapter,
I felt that I too belonged in there.

You handed me a quill, to fulfil
my heart's desire and let myself in.

I was no more the person I used to be,
It was only for you now that I existed.

Every part that I played in your life,
Got printed on my heart, deep inside.

Then one day you shut yourself up,
Try as I may, you wouldn't let me look.

Your cover became too heavy,
Refused to be opened by me.

Each time I tried to turn a leaf,
I'd be filled with the grief of defeat.

Every time I tried to write myself up,
I left with a deep paper-cut.

The cut was on my heart, not skin,
So, tried all I could, it never healed.

SEPARATION

I had you on my mind
But had not me in yours

I had your name in my words
But had not mine on your tongue

I had you in my arms
But had not me in your heart

I had you in my heart
But you'd have mine no more

Then it was time to let go
As you had already, long before.

TEARY EYED

We were friends once,
But no more so.

We were pals once,
Not so long ago.

Now she does not
Want me in her life.

Why then does she look
At me with teary eyes?

THE FIRST AND THE LAST

For many years, I remember,
Having a hollow space in my heart.
For many years, I remember,
Wanting to fill the space up fast.
For many years, I remember,
Wanting someone next to me at night.
For many years, I remember,
Wanting that bright beautiful smile.

For many years now, I've been trying,
To empty a place in my heart.
For many years now, I've been trying,
To fill it with someone else, at last.
For many years now, I've been trying,
To get you out of my dreams.
For many years now, I've been trying,
To forget the most beautiful smile I'd seen.

COME BACK

When the day is done
And the night is dry & cold,
Come back to me my love
Come back to me once more.

ETERNAL

Loved, you, me immensely,
Love you will, promised, for eternity;

Why love then, you stopped lovin' me,
Made promises never meant to keep?

FALLING

Falling in love,
One look at a time;
Love for you runs through my veins,
You are the one in my speech
And on my mind.

Each time I look at you,
I wish you loved me too;
But the thought I know
Is only in my heart,
Never crossed your mind.

NEVER

Never shall I ask to kiss you,
Nor think myself able enough to touch you.
For if I shall commit the crime,
Of passion with you.
Punished, under the verdict of love, I shall be,
For an eternity, and beyond that too.

OBLIGATIONS

I kept smiling for you,
you kept smiling for me;

Whereas all we wanted to do
was to break down and weep.

SHADOW

I sat in your shadow and wondered,
why it remained when you left.

NAKED

I stood there naked
He slowly faded,

I felt the cold wind
On my each limb,

My throat went dry
I almost began to cry,

I stood there waiting
Away he kept pacing,

I stood there still
With sorrow did my heart fill,

His image still appeared blurred
As I stood exposed to the world,

My mind as fragile as could be
The tears flowed down by cheeks,

The tears now fell on my breasts
But he kept marching without a rest,

Broken I was, flushed with dejection
An evil shadow walked steady in my direction,

I heard the evil shadow's chuckles
Stressed, I began to crack my knuckles,

I stood there terrified
Screaming and shouting inside,

I cried for him to stop and come back
He kept walking & the room on me turned
black.

UNHEARD

We met after seven years,
I told him I loved him, always had.
He asked me, why I hadn't said it
When he had said.

Perplexed, I asked when was that,
He told me he'd whispered,
In my ear, the last night we were together.
"I whispered in your ear,
when you were holding my hand,
your eyes were shut."

I asked him "which ear?",
He said he couldn't remember.
It hit us both then,
(I never heard him say he loved me,
How could I have?)

A deep sigh escaped his chest,
As he answered "left".
I am deaf in my left ear,
For the past ten years.
He is married now,
For the past seven.

TORRENTIAL TORMENT

I don't want to go and leave you in pain,
But I cannot stay and suffer the strain,
I want you to let me, I have to leave again.

HEART OF SHAME

My heart broke in two and went on war
My Heart of Shame vs. My Heart of Love;

One half of my heart put a dagger across
The other, and shouted, "Have Shame!"
My Heart of Love came ahead and gave
My Heart of Shame a long embrace
And whispered in its ear, "Have Strength."

Now in my chest I carry a heart,
Heavy with love, and with it, its shame;

Because in the most difficult of all battles,
Both the parts of my heart lost together
As the whole of my heart lost to your love.

IF

If someone were to ask me
Had I ever been in love
I would, without hesitation
Tell them that I am, right now.

That right at this moment,
I am in love with this woman
This wonderful woman I love
I love everything about her.

I love her smile
That wide open grin
I love her cute teeth
Love her luscious lips

I love her impatience
When things don't go right
I love her irritation when
She doesn't get the right reply

I love her jokes
I love her laughter
I love her dirty mind
I love her pure heart

I love her truths
I love her lies

I love her hair
I love her eyes

I love her body
Her presence
I love her skin
The texture of her touch

Yes, I am in love
I love this woman I am with
This wonderful woman I love
I love everything about her.

TASTED RED

I had looked at it, time and again,
In peoples' glasses and in peoples' hands.

There were two of a kind, Red and White,
But myself, I had never tasted Wine.

They said it gave warmth in cold winter
nights,
That it helped relax your nerves after tense
fights.

I had held a glass in my hands before,
Had only looked at it, nothing more.

A Sunday morning, I entered the forbidden
zone,
From the cellar downstairs, took a bottle of my
own.

There was Red, and there was White,
Something told me, Red would be just right.

I poured a drink, and let it touch my lips,
The taste, the warmth, it was pure bliss.

I let it flow inside me, from the bottle whole,
Before it was over, I wanted more.

Two, then three, bottles of wine I downed,
Before I knew, in Red I drowned.

I tasted White, but it did not compare,
I knew I tasted Wine, when I tasted Red.

SHE

She came into my world, uninvited,
Crept into my bed, unabashed;

She stared at me for long hours, unapologetic,
Dug her fingernails on my back, unabated;

She put her face to my neck, unpredicted,
Kissed it thrice softly, unpersuaded;

She declared her love for me, unpigmented,
She made me experience a love, unparalleled.

STEPS - A RHYME

One, Two;
Unbuckle your shoe,

Three, Four;
Lock the door,

Five, Six;
Let's click some pics,

Seven, Eight;
I can't think straight,

Nine, Ten;
Let's get it on then,

Eleven, Twelve;
Throw the clothes on the shelf,

Thirteen, Fourteen;
Forget the courting,

Fifteen, Sixteen;
It's getting obscene,

Seventeen, Eighteen:
Enter a world unseen,

Nineteen, Twenty;
Stop! we've done it plenty.

WHISPERS

What is it that you whisper in my ear?
It reaches my soul & doesn't even stop there!

VIRGIN

Every time I met you,
My heart felt flushed.
Each time like a virgin,
Still untouched.

LOVE AGAIN

When at night at 3am,
I suddenly awoke and
Said your name;
It is then that I knew,
I was in love again.

SONGBIRD

A songbird lived in my heart
It sang every time I cried
And made me feel better
The songbird was your smile.

SEASONS' MEETINGS

I met you in the summer sweet,
When the sun shined bright on the shrine;
I looked at you and asked your name,
You looked at me, then turned away and
smiled.

I met you when it started to rain,
The petrichor had filled the air;
I offered my umbrella and asked your name,
You took the umbrella and left in a flair.

I met you in autumn auburn,
When it rained leaves on the ground;
I turned to you and asked your name,
You looked at me, then looked away and
frowned.

It was winter when I met you next,
Each of us was in woollens, socks, mittens;
I looked at you and asked your name,
You looked at me and stood there smitten.

It was Spring when we met last like this,
The flowers then bloomed on every street;
I looked at you, you looked at me,
Then handed me a note done neat.

I read the note again and again;
In all the times I'd asked your name,
It had never once occurred to me,
You couldn't tell because you couldn't speak.

ORIENTAL BLOOM

It came into my dream,
A lush colourful plume;

It shone like the sun in the day,
At night it shone like a moon;

It smelled of a million roses,
Of mud and sandalwood;

It gave a scent, to me yet unknown,
Unknown, the feeling it gave me, too;

Its colour was dark like the night,
But also, bright, like white light;

Its colour, at times, it looked red,
At times a darker hue, who could tell;

Its texture, it seemed like a mix of few,
Unknown, the feeling it gave me, too;

It came into my dream,
A lush colourful plume;

It gave me a feeling,
That I cannot subdue.

BENEATH THE BANYAN TREE

You and I had walked together,
You and I had talked forever.

With you I was walking long, in glee,
Long you were walking with me.

With us the stars were walking,
The moon followed us, stalking.

The birds they went back to their nest,
The owls, that night, did not rest.

All night they hooted long and strong,
For us they sang a secret love-song.

The nightingale came and set the tone,
For a love that yet seemed forlorn.

The *Rajnigandha*, it filled our souls,
The *Anar* once more felt ripe and whole.

The dirt was soft, dark and moist,
The Banyan tree in it stood poised.

You and I, we looked in each-other's eyes,
Together then we looked at it, surmised.

You and I both wanted to sit beneath,
You and I both never wanted to leave.

So, on the eve of October twenty-three,
You and I sat beneath The Banyan Tree.

HEAVEN

I left the train at the station,
Was walking back home;
She caught on and walked next to me,
When she saw me walking alone

We walked for a while together,
The lane began to get narrow;
Her fingers brushed against mine,
Something in my heart fluttered, like a
sparrow

She walked on still, beside me,
Did not say a word;
Just when I thought I'd say something
The road hit a curve

I saw my house in the distance,
Couldn't believe, it was time already, to go!
With a heavy heart when I began to leave,
She smiled and said, "see you tomorrow!"

The sun seemed to rise that day,
In the evening at half past seven;
Standing in a dark, dingy lane in Bombay
Felt like being in heaven.

LOVERS' STORY

We hold hands and stroll in the alley,
When we die, they will make
A love shrine for us down the valley.

There were Romeo and Juliet,
And then the two of us will be
Forever alive, in the pages of History.

* 9 7 8 9 3 5 4 2 7 4 4 1 1 *

MAN - #0463 - 230726 - C0 - 203/127/3 - PB - 9789354274411 - Matt Lamination